Table of Contents

Blissful Bars

Cobbled Fruit Bars

1½ cups apple juice
 1 cup (6 ounces) chopped dried apricots
 1 cup (6 ounces) raisins
 1 package (6 ounces) dried cherries
 1 teaspoon cornstarch
 1 teaspoon ground cinnamon
 1 package (about 18 ounces) yellow cake mix
 2 cups old-fashioned oats
 ¾ cup (1½ sticks) butter, melted
 1 egg

1. Combine apple juice, apricots, raisins, cherries, cornstarch and cinnamon
in medium saucepan, stirring until cornstarch is dissolved. Bring to a boil over
medium heat. Boil 5 minutes, stirring constantly. Remove from heat; cool to room
temperature.

2. Preheat oven to 350°F. Line 15×10-inch jelly-roll pan with foil and spray lightly
with cooking spray.

3. Combine cake mix and oats in large bowl; stir in butter (mixture may be dry and
clumpy). Add egg; stir until well blended.

4. Press three fourths of dough mixture into prepared pan. Spread fruit mixture evenly
over top. Sprinkle remaining dough mixture over fruit. Bake 25 to 30 minutes or until
edges and top are lightly browned. Cool completely in pan on wire rack. Cut into bars.

Makes about 1 dozen bars

Double-Chocolate Pecan Brownies

¾ cup all-purpose flour
¾ cup unsweetened cocoa powder
½ cup CREAM OF WHEAT® Hot Cereal (Instant, 1-minute, 2½-minute
   or 10-minute cook time), uncooked
½ teaspoon baking powder
1¼ cups sugar
½ cup (1 stick) butter, softened
2 eggs
1 teaspoon vanilla extract
½ cup semisweet chocolate chips
½ cup pecans, chopped

1. Preheat oven to 350°F. Line 8-inch square baking pan with foil, extending
foil over sides of pan; spray with nonstick cooking spray. Combine flour, cocoa,
Cream of Wheat and baking powder in medium bowl; set aside.

2. Cream sugar and butter in large mixing bowl with electric mixer at medium speed.
Add eggs and vanilla; mix until well combined.

3. Gradually add Cream of Wheat mixture; mix well. Spread batter evenly in pan
with spatula. Sprinkle chocolate chips and pecans evenly over top.

4. Bake 35 minutes. Let stand 5 minutes. Lift brownies from pan using aluminum foil.
Cool completely before cutting.   *Makes 9 brownies*

Tip: For an even more decadent dessert, drizzle caramel sauce over the warm brownies
and serve with mint chocolate chip ice cream.

Prep Time: 15 minutes
Start to Finish Time: 1 hour

Double-Chocolate Pecan Brownies

Double-Decker Confetti Brownies

¾ cup (1½ sticks) butter or margarine, softened
1 cup granulated sugar
1 cup firmly packed light brown sugar
3 eggs
1 teaspoon vanilla extract
2½ cups all-purpose flour, divided
2½ teaspoons baking powder
½ teaspoon salt
⅓ cup unsweetened cocoa powder
1 tablespoon butter or margarine, melted
1 cup "M&M's"® Semi-Sweet Chocolate Mini Baking Bits, divided

Preheat oven to 350°F. Lightly grease 13×9×2-inch baking pan; set aside. In large bowl, cream ¾ cup butter and sugars until light and fluffy; beat in eggs and vanilla. In medium bowl, combine 2¼ cups flour, baking powder and salt; blend into creamed mixture. Divide batter in half. Blend together cocoa powder and melted butter; stir into one half of the dough. Spread cocoa dough evenly into prepared baking pan. Stir remaining ¼ cup flour and ½ cup "M&M's"® Semi-Sweet Chocolate Mini Baking Bits into remaining dough; spread evenly over cocoa dough in pan. Sprinkle with remaining ½ cup "M&M's"® Semi-Sweet Chocolate Mini Baking Bits. Bake 25 to 30 minutes or until edges start to pull away from sides of pan. Cool completely. Cut into bars. Store in tightly covered container.   *Makes 24 brownies*

Easy Microwave Brownies

1 cup granulated sugar
½ cup vegetable oil
¼ cup packed brown sugar
2 eggs
2 tablespoons corn syrup
1½ teaspoons vanilla
1 cup all-purpose flour
½ cup unsweetened cocoa powder
¼ teaspoon baking powder
¼ teaspoon salt
½ cup powdered sugar

Microwave Directions

1. Lightly grease 8-inch square microwavable dish.

2. Combine granulated sugar, oil, brown sugar, eggs, corn syrup and vanilla in large bowl. Combine flour, cocoa, baking powder and salt in medium bowl. Add flour mixture to sugar mixture; blend well. Spread batter in prepared dish.

3. Microwave on MEDIUM-HIGH (70%) 3 minutes. Rotate pan; microwave 3 minutes or until brownies begin to pull away from sides of pan and surface is dry. (If brownies are not done, rotate pan, turn and continue to microwave, checking for doneness at 30-second intervals.) Let brownies stand 20 minutes. When cool, sprinkle with powdered sugar and cut into squares. *Makes about 1 dozen brownies*

Black Forest Bars

  1 package (about 18 ounces) dark chocolate cake mix
½ cup (1 stick) unsalted butter, melted
  1 egg
½ teaspoon almond extract
  1 cup sliced almonds, divided
  1 jar (about 16 ounces) maraschino cherries, well drained
½ cup semisweet chocolate chips

1. Preheat oven to 350°F. Line 13×9-inch baking pan with foil; set aside.

2. Combine cake mix, butter, egg and extract in large bowl with electric mixer at medium speed. Stir in ¾ cup almonds.

3. Press dough into bottom of prepared pan. Top evenly with cherries. Bake 20 to 25 minutes or until toothpick inserted into center comes out clean. Cool completely in pan on wire rack.

4. Place chocolate chips in small resealable food storage bag; seal bag. Microwave on HIGH 1 to 1½ minutes, kneading bag every 30 seconds until melted and smooth. Cut tiny corner from bag; drizzle chocolate over brownies. Sprinkle with reserved almonds. Cut into bars. *Makes about 2 dozen bars*

Prep Time: 10 minutes
Bake Time: 20 to 25 minutes

Black Forest Bars

Double Peanut Butter Paisley Brownies

½ cup (1 stick) butter or margarine, softened
¼ cup REESE'S® Creamy Peanut Butter
1 cup granulated sugar
1 cup packed light brown sugar
3 eggs
1 teaspoon vanilla extract
2 cups all-purpose flour
2 teaspoons baking powder
¼ teaspoon salt
1⅔ cups (10-ounce package) REESE'S® Peanut Butter Chips
½ cup HERSHEY¿S Syrup or HERSHEY¿S SPECIAL DARK® Syrup

1. Heat oven to 350°F. Grease 13×9×2-inch baking pan.

2. Beat butter and peanut butter in large bowl. Add granulated sugar and brown sugar; beat well. Add eggs, one at a time, beating well after each addition. Blend in vanilla.

3. Stir together flour, baking powder and salt; mix into peanut butter mixture, blending well. Stir in peanut butter chips. Spread half of batter in prepared pan; spoon syrup over top. Carefully spread with remaining batter; swirl with metal spatula or knife for marbled effect.

4. Bake 35 to 40 minutes or until lightly browned. Cool completely in pan on wire rack. Cut into squares. *Makes about 36 brownies*

Double Peanut Butter Paisley Brownies

Coconut Key Lime Bars

1 package (about 18 ounces) white cake mix
1 cup toasted coconut, plus additional for garnish
½ cup (1 stick) butter, melted
1 can (14 ounces) sweetened condensed milk
1 package (8 ounces) cream cheese, softened
Grated peel and juice of 3 limes
3 eggs

1. Preheat oven to 350°F. Line 13×9-inch pan with foil, leaving 2-inch overhang on sides.

2. Beat cake mix, coconut and butter in large bowl with electric mixer at medium speed until crumbly. Press mixture into bottom of prepared pan. Bake 12 minutes or until light golden brown.

3. Beat sweetened condensed milk, cream cheese, lime peel and juice in another large bowl at medium speed 2 minutes or until well blended; scrape down sides of bowl. Beat in eggs one at a time. Spread mixture evenly over crust.

4. Bake 20 minutes or until filling is set and edges are lightly browned. Sprinkle with toasted coconut. Cool completely in pan on wire rack.   *Makes about 2 dozen bars*

Prep Time: 10 minutes
Bake Time: 40 to 45 minutes

The full flavor of shredded coconut is released when it is toasted. Spread the coconut in an even layer on a baking sheet and place it in a preheated 350°F oven for 5 to 7 minutes. Peek at it after 5 minutes to make sure it is not in any danger of burning. If the coconut is fresh and moist, it will take a little longer to toast to a nice golden color than drier coconut.

Chewy Peanut Butter Brownies

¾ cup (1½ sticks) butter, melted
¾ cup creamy peanut butter
1¾ cups sugar
2 teaspoons vanilla
4 eggs, lightly beaten
1¼ cups all-purpose flour
½ teaspoon baking powder
¼ teaspoon salt
¼ cup unsweetened cocoa powder

1. Preheat oven to 350°F. Grease 13×9-inch baking pan.

2. Beat butter and peanut butter in large bowl with electric mixer at low speed 3 minutes or until well blended. Add sugar and vanilla; beat until blended. Add eggs; beat until blended. Stir in flour, baking powder and salt just until blended. Reserve 1¾ cups batter. Stir cocoa into remaining batter.

3. Spread chocolate batter in prepared pan. Top with reserved batter. Bake 30 minutes or until edges begin to pull away from sides of pan. Cool completely in pan on wire rack. Cut into bars. *Makes 1½ dozen brownies*

Cran-Orange Oatmeal Bars

½ cup dried cranberries
½ cup (1 stick) butter, softened
1 egg
1 teaspoon grated orange peel, divided
3 tablespoons orange juice, divided
1 package (about 17 ounces) oatmeal cookie mix
1 cup powdered sugar

1. Preheat oven to 375°F. Spray 13×9-inch baking dish with nonstick cooking spray.

2. Combine cranberries, butter, egg, ½ teaspoon orange peel and 1 tablespoon juice in medium bowl. Stir in cookie mix until blended. Spread batter evenly in prepared dish.

3. Bake 17 minutes or until light golden brown around edges. Cool completely in pan on wire rack. Combine powdered sugar and remaining 2 tablespoons orange juice in small bowl; stir until smooth. Stir in remaining ½ teaspoon orange peel. Drizzle evenly over bars. *Makes about 2 dozen bars*

Chewy Peanut Butter Brownies

Sinful Cakes

German Upside Down Cake

1½ cups flaked coconut
1 cup chopped pecans
1 container (16 ounces) coconut pecan frosting
1 package (about 18 ounces) German chocolate cake mix
1⅓ cups water
1 cup milk chocolate chips
4 eggs
⅓ cup vegetable oil
Whipped cream (optional)

1. Preheat oven to 350°F. Spray 13×9-inch glass baking dish with nonstick cooking spray.

2. Spread coconut evenly in prepared pan. Sprinkle pecans over coconut. Spoon frosting by tablespoonfuls over pecans. (Do not spread.)

3. Beat cake mix, water, chocolate chips, eggs and oil in large bowl with electric mixer at low speed 30 seconds. Beat at medium speed 2 minutes or until well blended and smooth. Pour batter into prepared pan, spreading carefully over frosting. Bake 35 to 40 minutes or until toothpick inserted into center comes out clean. Cool in pan 10 minutes; invert onto serving plate. Serve warm; top with whipped cream.

Makes 16 to 18 servings

Cherry-Almond Streusel Cake

Cake
- 1½ cups biscuit baking mix
- ½ cup milk
- 2 eggs
- 2 tablespoons granulated sugar
- 2 tablespoons vegetable oil
- 1 teaspoon vanilla
- ¼ teaspoon almond extract
- ½ to ¾ cup dried cherries*

Topping
- ½ cup slivered almonds
- ½ cup oats
- ⅓ cup biscuit baking mix
- ⅓ cup packed dark brown sugar
- ¼ teaspoon ground cinnamon
- 3 tablespoons cold butter, cubed

*Any dried fruit, such as cranberries or raisins, may be substituted.

1. Preheat oven to 375°F. Spray 8-inch round baking pan with nonstick cooking spray.

2. Combine 1½ cups baking mix, milk, eggs, granulated sugar, oil, vanilla and almond extract in medium bowl. Stir until well blended. Gently stir in cherries. Spread batter into prepared pan; set aside.

3. Combine almonds, oats, ⅓ cup baking mix, brown sugar and cinnamon in medium bowl. Cut in butter with pastry blender or two knives until mixture is crumbly.

4. Sprinkle topping evenly over batter. Bake 18 to 20 minutes or until toothpick inserted into center comes out almost clean. Let stand at least 30 minutes before serving.

Makes 12 servings

Cherry-Almond Streusel Cake

Chocolate Lemon Marble Cake

2½ cups all-purpose flour
1¾ cups plus ⅓ cup sugar, divided
2 teaspoons baking powder
1¼ teaspoons baking soda, divided
½ teaspoon salt
⅓ cup butter or margarine, softened
⅓ cup shortening
3 eggs
1⅔ cups buttermilk or sour milk*
2 teaspoons vanilla extract
⅓ cup HERSHEY'S Cocoa
¼ cup water
2 teaspoons freshly grated lemon peel
¼ teaspoon lemon juice
Cocoa Glaze (page 22)

To sour milk: Use 1 tablespoon plus 2 teaspoons white vinegar plus milk to equal 1⅔ cups.

1. Heat oven to 375°F. Grease and flour 12-cup fluted tube pan.**

2. Stir together flour, 1¾ cups sugar, baking powder, 1 teaspoon baking soda and salt in large bowl. Add butter, shortening, eggs, buttermilk and vanilla; beat on medium speed of electric mixer 3 minutes.

3. Stir together cocoa, remaining ⅓ cup sugar, remaining ¼ teaspoon baking soda and water; blend into ⅔ cup vanilla batter. Blend lemon peel and lemon juice into remaining vanilla batter; drop spoonfuls of lemon batter into prepared pan. Drop spoonfuls of chocolate batter on top of lemon batter; swirl with knife or metal spatula for marbled effect.

4. Bake 35 to 40 minutes or until wooden pick inserted into center comes out clean. Cool 15 minutes; remove from pan to wire rack. Cool completely. Glaze with Cocoa Glaze. *Makes 16 to 18 servings*

**Cake may also be baked in two 9×5×3-inch loaf pans. Bake 40 to 45 minutes or until wooden pick inserted into center comes out clean.*

continued on page 22

Chocolate Lemon Marble Cake

Chocolate Lemon Marble Cake, continued

Cocoa Glaze

- ¼ cup **HERSHEY'S Cocoa**
- 3 tablespoons light corn syrup
- 4 teaspoons water
- ½ teaspoon vanilla extract
- 1 cup powdered sugar

Combine cocoa, corn syrup and water in small saucepan; cook over medium heat, stirring constantly, until mixture thickens. Remove from heat; blend in vanilla and powdered sugar. Beat until smooth. *Makes about 1½ cups*

Sweet and Sour Brunch Cake

- 1 package (16 ounces) frozen rhubarb or unsweetened strawberries, thawed and patted dry
- 1 cup packed brown sugar
- 1 tablespoon all-purpose flour
- 1 teaspoon ground cinnamon
- ¼ cup (½ stick) butter, cut into small pieces
- 1 package (about 18 ounces) yellow cake mix *without* pudding in the mix
- 1 package (4-serving size) vanilla instant pudding and pie filling mix
- 4 eggs
- ⅔ cup sour cream
- ½ cup water
- ½ cup vegetable oil

1. Preheat oven to 350°F. Spray 13×9-inch baking pan with nonstick cooking spray.

2. Spread rhubarb evenly in single layer in prepared pan. Combine brown sugar, flour and cinnamon in small bowl; mix well. Sprinkle evenly over rhubarb; dot with butter.

3. Beat cake mix, pudding mix, eggs, sour cream, water and oil in large bowl with electric mixer at low speed 1 minute. Beat at medium speed 2 minutes or until well blended and creamy. Pour batter into prepared pan; spread carefully over rhubarb mixture.

4. Bake 40 to 50 minutes or until toothpick inserted into center comes out clean.

Makes 16 to 18 servings

Sweet and Sour Brunch Cake

Oat-Apricot Snack Cake

  1 (8-ounce) container plain yogurt (not fat free)
  ¾ cup packed brown sugar
  ½ cup granulated sugar
  ⅓ cup vegetable oil
  1 egg
  2 tablespoons milk
  2 teaspoons vanilla
  1 cup all-purpose flour
  ½ cup whole wheat flour
  1 teaspoon baking soda
  1 teaspoon cinnamon
  ½ teaspoon salt
  2 cups old-fashioned oats
  1 cup (about 6 ounces) chopped dried apricots
  1 cup powdered sugar
  2 tablespoons milk

1. Preheat oven to 350°F. Spray 13×9-inch baking pan with nonstick cooking spray. Stir yogurt, sugars, oil, egg, milk and vanilla in large bowl until thoroughly mixed.

2. Sift flours, baking soda, cinnamon and salt in medium bowl. Add dry ingredients to wet ingredients; mix well. Stir in oats and apricots until well blended.

3. Spread batter in prepared pan. Bake 25 to 30 minutes or until toothpick inserted into center comes out clean. Cool completely in pan on wire rack.

4. Stir powdered sugar and milk in small bowl until smooth. Spoon glaze into small resealable food storage bag. Seal bag and cut ¼ inch from one corner; drizzle glaze over bars. *Makes 16 to 18 servings*

Cranberry Pound Cake

  1½ cups sugar
  1 cup (2 sticks) unsalted butter
  ¼ teaspoon salt
  ¼ teaspoon ground nutmeg or mace
  4 eggs
  2 cups cake flour
  1 cup chopped fresh or frozen cranberries

1. Preheat oven to 350°F. Grease and flour 9×5-inch loaf pan.

2. Beat sugar, butter, salt and nutmeg in large bowl with electric mixer at medium speed until light and fluffy. Beat in eggs, one at a time, until well blended. Reduce speed to low; add flour, ½ cup at a time, scraping down bowl occasionally. Fold in cranberries.

3. Spoon batter into prepared pan. Bake 60 to 70 minutes or until toothpick inserted into center comes out clean. Cool in pan on wire rack 5 minutes. Run knife around edges of pan to loosen cake; cool additional 30 minutes. Remove from pan; cool completely on wire rack. *Makes 12 servings*

Pistachio Walnut Bundt Cake

> 1 package (about 18 ounces) white cake mix *without* pudding in the mix
> 1 package (4-serving size) pistachio instant pudding and pie filling mix
> 1 cup water
> 3 eggs
> 2 teaspoons ground cinnamon
> ½ cup chopped walnuts
> Powdered sugar (optional)

1. Preheat oven to 325°F. Spray 12-cup bundt pan with nonstick cooking spray.

2. Beat cake mix, pudding mix, water, eggs and cinnamon in large bowl with electric mixer at medium-high speed 2 minutes or until blended. Stir in walnuts. Pour into prepared pan.

3. Bake 40 to 50 minutes or until cake springs back when lightly touched. Cool in pan on wire rack 10 minutes. Invert cake onto serving plate; cool completely. Sprinkle with powdered sugar. *Makes 12 to 16 servings*

Double Chocolate Chip Snack Cake

1 package (about 18 ounces) devil's food cake mix
  with pudding in the mix, divided
2 eggs
½ cup water
¼ cup vegetable oil
½ teaspoon cinnamon
1 cup semisweet chocolate chips, divided
¼ cup packed brown sugar
2 tablespoons butter, melted
¾ cup white chocolate chips

1. Preheat oven to 350°F. Grease 9-inch round cake pan. Reserve ¾ cup dry cake mix.

2. Beat remaining cake mix, eggs, water, oil and cinnamon in large bowl with electric mixer at medium speed 2 minutes. Remove ½ cup batter; reserve for another use.* Spread remaining batter in prepared pan; sprinkle with ½ cup semisweet chocolate chips.

3. Combine reserved cake mix and brown sugar in medium bowl. Stir in butter and remaining semisweet chocolate chips; mix well. Sprinkle mixture over batter in pan.

4. Bake 35 to 40 minutes or until toothpick inserted into center comes out clean and cake springs back when lightly touched. Cool cake in pan on wire rack 10 minutes. Remove to wire rack; cool completely.

5. Place white chocolate chips in medium resealable food storage bag; seal bag. Microwave on HIGH 10 seconds and knead bag gently. Repeat until chips are melted. Cut off ¼ inch from corner of bag; drizzle chocolate over cake. Let glaze set before cutting into wedges. *Makes 8 to 10 servings*

If desired, extra batter can be used for cupcakes. Pour batter into two foil baking cups placed on baking sheet. Bake at 350°F 18 to 20 minutes or until toothpick inserted into centers comes out clean.

Double Chocolate Chip Snack Cake

Honey-Orange Spicecake

¾ **cup honey**
⅓ **cup oil**
¼ **cup orange juice**
2 **eggs**
1½ **cups all-purpose flour**
1 **teaspoon baking powder**
1 **teaspoon ground cinnamon**
½ **teaspoon baking soda**
¼ **teaspoon ground cloves**

Orange Syrup
¼ **cup honey**
¼ **cup orange juice**
2 **teaspoons freshly grated orange peel**

Using electric mixer, beat together honey, oil and orange juice; beat in eggs. Combine dry ingredients; gradually add to honey mixture, mixing until well blended.

Pour into lightly greased and floured 9×9-inch baking pan. Bake at 350°F for 25 to 30 minutes or until toothpick inserted in center comes out clean. Meanwhile, make syrup. In small saucepan, combine honey, orange juice and peel. Bring just to a boil. Remove cake from oven and immediately cut into squares.

Pour hot syrup evenly over cake in pan. Cool in pan on wire rack.

Makes 9 servings

Favorite recipe from **National Honey Board**

Butterscotch Bundt Cake

- 1 package (about 18 ounces) yellow cake mix *without* pudding in the mix
- 1 package (4-serving size) butterscotch instant pudding and pie filling mix
- 1 cup water
- 3 eggs
- 2 teaspoons ground cinnamon
- ½ cup chopped pecans
  Powdered sugar (optional)

1. Preheat oven to 325°F. Spray 12-cup bundt pan with nonstick cooking spray.

2. Beat cake mix, pudding mix, water, eggs and cinnamon in large bowl with electric mixer at medium-high speed 2 minutes or until blended. Stir in pecans. Pour into prepared pan.

3. Bake 40 to 50 minutes or until cake springs back when lightly touched. Cool in pan on wire rack 10 minutes. Invert cake onto serving plate; cool completely. Sprinkle with powdered sugar.

Makes 12 to 16 servings

Mandarin Orange Tea Cake

- 1 package (about 16 ounces) pound cake mix
- ½ cup plus 2 tablespoons orange juice, divided
- 2 eggs
- ¼ cup milk
- 1 can (15 ounces) mandarin orange segments in light syrup, drained
- ¾ cup powdered sugar
  Grated peel of 1 orange

1. Preheat oven to 350°F. Grease 9-inch bundt pan.

2. Beat cake mix, ½ cup orange juice, eggs and milk in large bowl with electric mixer at medium speed 2 minutes or until light and fluffy. Fold in orange segments. Pour batter into prepared pan.

3. Bake 45 minutes or until golden brown and toothpick inserted near center comes out clean. Cool in pan 15 minutes on wire rack. Invert cake onto rack; cool completely.

4. Combine sugar, orange peel and remaining 2 tablespoons orange juice in small bowl; stir until smooth. Drizzle glaze over cake. Allow glaze to set about 5 minutes before serving.

Makes 16 servings

Butterscotch Bundt Cake

Chocolate Crispy Treat Cake

1 package (about 18 ounces) chocolate fudge cake mix,
    plus ingredients to prepare mix
1 cup semisweet chocolate chips
¼ cup light corn syrup
¼ cup (½ stick) butter
½ cup powdered sugar
2 cups crisp rice cereal
4 cups mini marshmallows (half of 10½-ounce package)

1. Preheat oven to 350°F. Grease bottom only of 13×9-inch pan. Prepare cake mix according to package directions; pour into prepared pan. Bake 25 to 30 minutes or until cake is set.

2. Meanwhile, heat chocolate chips, corn syrup and butter in medium saucepan over low heat, stirring frequently, until chocolate and butter are melted. Remove from heat; blend in powdered sugar. Gently stir in cereal until well blended.

3. Remove cake from oven; sprinkle marshmallows over top of cake in single layer. Return cake to oven; bake 2 to 3 minutes longer until marshmallows puff up slightly.

4. Spread chocolate cereal mixture over marshmallows. Let cake stand until set.

Makes 16 to 18 servings

Note: This cake is best eaten within a day or two of baking. After two days the cereal will become soggy.

Easy Apple Butter Cake

1 package (about 18 ounces) yellow cake mix *without* pudding in the mix
1 package (4-serving size) vanilla instant pudding and pie filling mix
1 cup sour cream
1 cup apple butter
4 eggs
½ cup apple juice
¼ cup vegetable oil
1 teaspoon ground cinnamon
½ teaspoon ground nutmeg
½ teaspoon ground cloves
¼ teaspoon salt
   Powdered sugar (optional)

1. Preheat oven to 375°F. Spray 10-inch tube pan with nonstick cooking spray.

2. Beat cake mix, pudding mix, sour cream, apple butter, eggs, apple juice, oil, cinnamon, nutmeg, cloves and salt in large bowl with electric mixer at low speed 1 minute. Beat at medium speed 2 minutes or until well blended and fluffy. Pour batter into prepared pan.

3. Bake 45 to 50 minutes or until toothpick inserted near center comes out clean. Cool in pan on wire rack 20 minutes. Run sharp knife along edge of pan to release cake; invert cake onto serving plate. Cool completely.

4. Just before serving, if desired, place 9-inch paper doily over cake. Sift powdered sugar over doily; remove carefully.   *Makes 12 servings*

A butter cake is done when it begins to pull away from the sides of the pan, the top springs back when lightly touched and a toothpick inserted into the center comes out clean and dry.

Cookie Jar

Chocolate Chunk Cookies

1⅔ cups all-purpose flour
⅓ cup CREAM OF WHEAT® Hot Cereal (Instant, 1-minute,
　　2½-minute or 10-minute cook time), uncooked
½ teaspoon baking soda
¼ teaspoon salt
¾ cup (1½ sticks) butter, softened
½ cup packed brown sugar
⅓ cup granulated sugar
1 egg
1 teaspoon vanilla extract
1 (11½-ounce) bag chocolate chunks
1 cup chopped pecans

1. Preheat oven to 375°F. Lightly grease cookie sheets. Blend flour, Cream of Wheat, baking soda and salt in medium bowl; set aside.

2. Beat butter and sugars in large bowl with electric mixer at medium speed until creamy. Add egg and vanilla. Beat until fluffy. Reduce speed to low. Add Cream of Wheat mixture; mix well. Stir in chocolate chunks and pecans.

3. Drop by tablespoonfuls onto prepared cookie sheets. Bake 9 to 11 minutes or until golden brown. Let stand on cookie sheet 1 minute before transferring to wire racks to cool completely. *Makes 24 cookies*

Tip: For a colorful item to take to school bake sales, replace the chocolate chunks with multicolored candy-coated chocolate.

Prep Time: 15 minutes
Start to Finish Time: 35 minutes

Peanut Butter Blossoms

48 **HERSHEY₂S KISSES®**ʙʀᴀɴᴅ **Milk Chocolates**
¾ **cup REESE'S® Creamy Peanut Butter**
½ **cup shortening**
⅓ **cup granulated sugar**
⅓ **cup packed light brown sugar**
1 **egg**
2 **tablespoons milk**
1 **teaspoon vanilla extract**
1½ **cups all-purpose flour**
1 **teaspoon baking soda**
½ **teaspoon salt**
 Granulated sugar

1. Heat oven to 375°F. Remove wrappers from chocolates.

2. Beat peanut butter and shortening with electric mixer on medium speed in large bowl until well blended. Add ⅓ cup granulated sugar and brown sugar; beat until fluffy. Add egg, milk and vanilla; beat well. Stir together flour, baking soda and salt; gradually beat into peanut butter mixture.

3. Shape dough into 1-inch balls. Roll in additional granulated sugar; place on ungreased cookie sheet.

4. Bake 8 to 10 minutes or until lightly browned. Immediately press a chocolate into center of each cookie; cookies will crack around edges. Remove to wire racks and cool completely. *Makes about 4 dozen cookies*

 Be creative at your next bake sale. Try placing the home-baked cookies on a decorative plate or in a gift box filled with colored tissue. Cookies can also be wrapped back-to-back in pairs with clear or colored plastic wrap and tied with colorful ribbon.

Coconut Clouds

   1 package (about 16 ounces) confetti angel food cake mix
  ½ cup water
 1½ cups sweetened flaked coconut
 1¼ cups slivered almonds, divided

1. Preheat oven to 325°F. Line cookie sheets with parchment paper.

2. Beat cake mix and water in large bowl with electric mixer at medium-high speed 3 minutes or until fluffy. Add coconut and 1 cup almonds; beat until combined. Drop tablespoonfuls of dough 2 inches apart onto prepared cookie sheets. Sprinkle tops with remaining ¼ cup almonds.

3. Bake 18 to 20 minutes or until bottoms are golden brown. Cool 1 minute on cookie sheets. Remove to wire rack to cool completely. *Makes 4 dozen cookies*

Prep Time: 10 minutes
Bake Time: 22 to 24 minutes

Chunky Oatmeal Raisin Cookies

   1 package (about 18 ounces) yellow cake mix
 1½ cups old-fashioned oats
  ½ cup all-purpose flour
  2 teaspoons ground cinnamon
  ½ cup packed brown sugar
  2 eggs
  1 teaspoon vanilla
  1 cup (2 sticks) unsalted butter, melted
  1 cup raisins
  1 cup walnut pieces, toasted

1. Preheat oven to 375°F. Line cookie sheets with parchment paper.

2. Combine cake mix, oats, flour and cinnamon in large bowl until well blended. Beat brown sugar, eggs and vanilla in medium bowl until well blended. Add egg mixture and butter to dry ingredients; stir until combined. Fold in raisins and walnuts.

3. Drop tablespoonfuls of dough 2 inches apart onto prepared cookie sheets. Bake 14 to 16 minutes or until bottoms are golden brown. *Makes about 4 dozen cookies*

Prep Time: 15 minutes
Bake Time: 14 minutes

Coconut Clouds

Greek Date-Nut Swirls

1 cup firmly packed dried figs
1 cup firmly packed pitted dates
1 cup coarsely chopped walnuts
12 tablespoons granulated sugar, divided
½ cup water
1¾ cups all-purpose flour
2 teaspoons ground anise seeds
¼ teaspoon baking powder
¼ teaspoon baking soda
¼ teaspoon salt
½ cup (1 stick) unsalted butter, softened
4 ounces cream cheese, softened
1 egg yolk
1 teaspoon vanilla

1. Combine figs, dates, walnuts, 3 tablespoons sugar and water in food processor or blender; process until smooth.

2. Stir together flour, anise, baking powder, baking soda and salt in medium bowl; set aside.

3. Beat butter, cream cheese and 3 tablespoons sugar with electric mixer at medium speed until light and creamy. Add egg yolk, vanilla and flour mixture; beat until soft dough forms. Form dough into disc; wrap tightly in plastic wrap. Refrigerate at least 2 hours or until firm.

4. Place sheet of waxed paper on smooth, dry surface. Roll dough into 13×10-inch rectangle with lightly floured rolling pin. Gently spread fig mixture in even layer over dough. Beginning on one long side, lift waxed paper to roll up dough jelly-roll style. Spread remaining 6 tablespoons sugar on another sheet of waxed paper; roll log in sugar. Wrap sugared log in plastic wrap; refrigerate until firm, at least 4 hours or overnight.

5. Preheat oven to 350°F. Line two cookie sheets with parchment paper. Cut log into ⅓-inch-thick slices. Place 2 inches apart on prepared cookie sheets.

6. Bake 12 to 14 minutes or until cookies are light golden brown. Cool 1 minute on cookie sheets; transfer to wire rack to cool completely. Store in airtight container.

Makes about 3 dozen cookies

Quick Peanut Butter Chocolate Chip Cookies

1 package **DUNCAN HINES® Moist Deluxe® Classic Yellow Cake Mix**
½ cup **creamy peanut butter**
½ cup **(1 stick) butter or margarine, softened**
2 **eggs**
1 cup **milk chocolate chips**

1. Preheat oven to 350°F. Grease baking sheets.

2. Combine cake mix, peanut butter, butter and eggs in large bowl. Beat at low speed with electric mixer until well blended. Stir in chocolate chips.

3. Drop by rounded teaspoonfuls onto prepared baking sheets. Bake at 350°F for 9 to 11 minutes or until lightly browned. Cool 2 minutes on baking sheets. Remove to cooling racks. *Makes about 4 dozen cookies*

Tip: Crunchy peanut butter can be substituted for creamy peanut butter.

Cinnamon-Sugar Knots

¼ cup **granulated sugar**
¾ teaspoon **ground cinnamon**
1 package **(about 18 ounces) spice cake mix**
1 package **(8 ounces) cream cheese, softened**

1. Preheat oven to 350°F. Combine sugar and cinnamon in small bowl; set aside.

2. Beat cake mix and cream cheese together in large bowl with electric mixer at medium speed until well blended.

3. Shape dough into 1-inch balls; roll each ball into log about 4 inches long. Gently coil dough and pull up ends to form knot. Place about 1½ inches apart on ungreased cookie sheets. Sprinkle with cinnamon-sugar. Bake 10 to 12 minutes or until edges are lightly browned.

4. Cool 2 minutes on cookie sheets. Remove to wire rack. Serve warm or cool completely before serving. *Makes about 4 dozen cookies*

Prep Time: 15 minutes
Bake Time: 10 to 12 minutes

Almond Milk Chocolate Chippers

1¼ **cups all-purpose flour**
½ **teaspoon baking soda**
½ **teaspoon salt**
½ **cup (1 stick) butter, softened**
½ **cup packed light brown sugar**
⅓ **cup granulated sugar**
1 **egg**
2 **tablespoons almond-flavored liqueur**
1 **cup milk chocolate chips**
½ **cup slivered almonds, toasted***

* To toast almonds, spread on baking sheet. Bake 5 to 7 minutes or until golden brown, stirring frequently.

1. Preheat oven to 375°F. Combine flour, baking soda and salt in small bowl.

2. Beat butter and sugars in large bowl with electric mixer at medium speed 2 to 3 minutes or until creamy. Beat in egg until well blended. Beat in liqueur. Gradually add flour mixture, beating until well blended. Stir in chips and almonds.

3. Drop dough by rounded teaspoonfuls 2 inches apart onto ungreased cookie sheets.

4. Bake 9 to 10 minutes or until edges are golden brown. Cool 2 minutes on cookie sheets. Remove to wire racks to cool completely. Store tightly covered at room temperature or freeze up to 3 months. *Makes about 3 dozen cookies*

Almond Milk Chocolate Chippers

Oatmeal Scotchies

1¼ cups all-purpose flour
1 teaspoon baking soda
½ teaspoon salt
½ teaspoon ground cinnamon
1 cup (2 sticks) butter or margarine, softened
¾ cup granulated sugar
¾ cup packed brown sugar
2 eggs
1 teaspoon vanilla extract *or* grated peel of 1 orange
3 cups quick or old-fashioned oats
1⅔ cups (11-ounce package) NESTLÉ® TOLL HOUSE® Butterscotch Flavored Morsels

PREHEAT oven to 375°F.

COMBINE flour, baking soda, salt and cinnamon in small bowl. Beat butter, granulated sugar, brown sugar, eggs and vanilla extract in large mixer bowl. Gradually beat in flour mixture. Stir in oats and morsels. Drop by rounded tablespoonfuls onto ungreased baking sheets.

BAKE for 7 to 8 minutes for chewy cookies or 9 to 10 minutes for crispy cookies. Cool on baking sheets for 2 minutes; remove to wire racks to cool completely.

Makes about 4 dozen cookies

Pan Cookie Variation: GREASE 15×10-inch jelly-roll pan. Spread dough into prepared pan. Bake for 18 to 22 minutes or until light brown. Cool completely in pan on wire rack. Makes 4 dozen bars.

Chocolate Cherry Gems

      1 package (about 16 ounces) refrigerated sugar cookie dough
    ⅓ cup unsweetened Dutch process cocoa powder*
      3 tablespoons maraschino cherry juice, divided
    18 maraschino cherries, cut in half
    ¾ cup powdered sugar

*Dutch process, or European-style, cocoa gives these cookies an intense chocolate flavor and a dark, rich color. Other unsweetened cocoa powders can be substituted, but the flavor may be milder and the color may be lighter.

1. Preheat oven to 350°F. Lightly grease cookie sheets. Let dough stand at room temperature about 15 minutes.

2. Beat dough, cocoa and 1 tablespoon cherry juice in large bowl until well blended. Shape dough into 36 (¾-inch) balls; place 2 inches apart on prepared cookie sheets. Flatten balls slightly; press cherry half into center of each ball.

3. Bake 9 to 11 minutes or until set. Cool 2 minutes on cookie sheets; remove to wire racks to cool completely.

4. Combine powdered sugar and remaining 2 tablespoons cherry juice in small bowl; whisk until smooth. Add additional juice, 1 teaspoon at a time, if necessary, to create medium-thick pourable glaze. Drizzle glaze over cooled cookies. Let stand until set.

Makes 3 dozen cookies

Chocolate Cherry Gems

Peanut Butter & Banana Cookies

¼ cup (½ stick) butter
½ cup mashed ripe banana
½ cup peanut butter
¼ cup frozen apple juice concentrate
1 egg
1 teaspoon vanilla
1 cup all-purpose flour
½ teaspoon baking soda
¼ teaspoon salt
½ cup chopped salted peanuts
   Whole salted peanuts (optional)

1. Preheat oven to 375°F. Grease cookie sheets.

2. Beat butter in large bowl until creamy. Add banana and peanut butter; beat until smooth. Blend in apple juice concentrate, egg and vanilla. Beat in flour, baking soda and salt. Stir in chopped peanuts.

3. Drop dough by rounded tablespoonfuls 2 inches apart onto prepared cookie sheets; top each with one whole peanut, if desired. Bake 8 minutes or until set. Cool completely on wire racks. Store in tightly covered container.

Makes 2 dozen cookies

To make apple juice from a partially used can of concentrate, measure the amount of remaining concentrate and then add three times that amount in water. Stir well and enjoy.

Tons of Muffins

Raspberry Streusel Muffins

Topping

- 1 cup sugar
- ⅔ cup all-purpose flour
- ¼ cup pecan chips
- 1 teaspoon cinnamon
- ¼ teaspoon salt
- ½ cup (1 stick) butter, cut into small pieces
- 1 tablespoon milk

Muffins

- 3 cups all-purpose flour
- 2 teaspoons baking powder
- ½ teaspoon salt
- ⅛ teaspoon ground cinnamon
- 1½ cups sugar
- ½ cup (1 stick) butter
- 2 eggs
- 1 teaspoon vanilla
- 1 cup sour cream
- 1½ pints fresh raspberries

1. Preheat oven to 350°F. Line 24 standard (2½-inch) muffin cups with paper baking cups.

2. For topping, combine sugar, flour, pecans, cinnamon and salt in medium bowl. Cut in butter and milk with pastry blender or two knives until mixture resembles coarse crumbs. Set aside.

continued on page 54

Raspberry Streusel Muffins, continued

3. For muffins, whisk flour, baking powder, salt and cinnamon in medium bowl. Set aside.

4. Beat sugar and butter in large bowl with electric mixer at medium speed 2 to 3 minutes or until light and fluffy. Add eggs, one at a time, beating well after each addition. Stir in vanilla. Mix in dry ingredients, alternating with sour cream. Gently fold in raspberries. Pour into muffin pans; sprinkle with topping.

5. Bake 20 to 25 minutes or until toothpick inserted into centers comes out clean. Cool pans on wire racks 10 minutes. Remove from pans; cool completely on racks.

Makes 24 muffins

Pumpkin Chocolate Chip Muffins

2½ **cups all-purpose flour**
1 **tablespoon baking powder**
1½ **teaspoons pumpkin pie spice***
½ **teaspoon salt**
1 **cup packed light brown sugar**
1 **cup solid-pack pumpkin (not pumpkin pie filling)**
¾ **cup milk**
6 **tablespoons butter, melted**
2 **eggs**
1 **cup semisweet chocolate chips**
½ **cup chopped walnuts**

*Or substitute ¾ teaspoon ground cinnamon, ⅜ teaspoon ground ginger and scant ¼ teaspoon each ground allspice and ground nutmeg.

1. Preheat oven to 400°F. Line 18 standard (2½-inch) muffin cups with paper baking cups or spray with nonstick cooking spray.

2. Combine flour, baking powder, pumpkin pie spice and salt in large bowl. Beat brown sugar, pumpkin, milk, butter and eggs in medium bowl until well blended. Add pumpkin mixture, chocolate chips and walnuts to flour mixture; stir just until moistened. Spoon evenly into prepared muffin cups, filling two-thirds full.

3. Bake 15 to 17 minutes or until toothpick inserted into centers comes out clean. Cool in pans on wire racks 10 minutes. Remove from pans to rack; cool completely.

Makes 18 muffins

Pumpkin Chocolate Chip Muffins

Cranberry Pecan Muffins

1¾ cups all-purpose flour
½ cup packed light brown sugar
2½ teaspoons baking powder
½ teaspoon salt
¾ cup milk
¼ cup (½ stick) butter, melted
1 egg, beaten
1 cup chopped fresh cranberries
⅓ cup chopped pecans
1 teaspoon grated lemon peel

1. Preheat oven to 400°F. Grease 36 mini (1¼-inch) muffin cups.

2. Combine flour, brown sugar, baking powder and salt in large bowl. Combine milk, butter and egg in small bowl until blended; stir into flour mixture just until moistened. Fold in cranberries, pecans and lemon peel. Spoon evenly into prepared muffin cups.

3. Bake 15 to 17 minutes or until toothpick inserted into centers comes out clean. Remove from pans; cool on wire racks.   *Makes 3 dozen mini muffins*

Red, White and Blue Muffins

2 cups all-purpose flour
¾ cup white chocolate chips
¾ cup *each* sweetened dried cranberries and dried blueberries
½ cup sugar
1 tablespoon baking powder
½ teaspoon salt
1 cup milk
½ cup (1 stick) butter, melted
1 egg, beaten
1 teaspoon vanilla

1. Preheat oven to 350°F. Grease 12 standard (2½-inch) muffin cups.

2. Combine flour, chocolate chips, dried berries, sugar, baking powder and salt in medium bowl. Combine milk, butter, egg and vanilla in large bowl. Add flour mixture to milk mixture; stir just until moistened. Spoon evenly into prepared muffin cups.

3. Bake 20 to 25 minutes or until toothpick inserted into centers comes out clean. Cool 10 minutes on wire rack.   *Makes 12 muffins*

Cranberry Pecan Muffins

Holiday Pumpkin Muffins

2½ **cups all-purpose flour**
1 **cup packed light brown sugar**
1 **tablespoon baking powder**
1 **teaspoon ground cinnamon**
½ **teaspoon ground nutmeg**
½ **teaspoon ground ginger**
¼ **teaspoon salt**
1 **cup solid-pack pumpkin (not pumpkin pie filling)**
¾ **cup milk**
2 **eggs**
6 **tablespoons butter, melted**
⅔ **cup roasted, salted pumpkin seeds, divided**
½ **cup golden raisins**

1. Preheat oven to 400°F. Grease 18 standard (2½-inch) muffin cups or line with paper baking cups.

2. Combine flour, brown sugar, baking powder, cinnamon, nutmeg, ginger and salt in large bowl. Stir pumpkin, milk, eggs and butter in medium bowl until well blended. Stir pumpkin mixture into flour mixture just until moistened. Stir in ⅓ cup pumpkin seeds and raisins. Spoon into prepared muffin cups, filling two-thirds full. Sprinkle remaining pumpkin seeds over muffin batter.

3. Bake 15 to 18 minutes or until toothpick inserted into center comes out clean. Cool in pans 10 minutes. Remove from pans and cool completely on wire racks. Store in airtight container. *Makes 18 muffins*

Carrot Pineapple Muffins

4 cups grated carrots (spooned, not packed, into cup)
1 cup granulated sugar
1 cup packed brown sugar
1 can (8 ounces) crushed pineapple in unsweetened pineapple juice, undrained
1 cup Dried Plum Purée (recipe follows) or prepared dried plum butter
4 egg whites
2 teaspoons vanilla
2 cups all-purpose flour
2 teaspoons baking soda
2 teaspoons ground cinnamon
½ teaspoon salt
¾ cup raisins (optional)

Preheat oven to 375°F. Coat eighteen 2¾-inch (⅓-cup capacity) muffin cups with vegetable cooking spray. In large bowl, beat carrots, sugars, pineapple, Dried Plum Purée, egg whites and vanilla until well blended. In medium bowl, combine flour, baking soda, cinnamon and salt. Add flour mixture to carrot mixture; mix just until blended. Stir in raisins. Spoon batter into prepared muffin cups, dividing equally. Bake in center of oven about 20 to 25 minutes or until springy to the touch and pick inserted into centers comes out clean. Cool in pans 15 minutes. Remove to wire racks. Serve warm. *Makes 18 muffins*

Plum Purée

1⅓ cups (8 ounces) pitted dried plums
6 tablespoons hot water

Combine plums and water in container of food processor or blender. Pulse on and off until dried plums are finely chopped and smooth. Store leftovers in covered container in refrigerator for up to two months. Makes 1 cup.

Favorite recipes from **California Dried Plum Board**

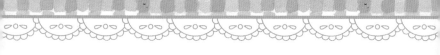

Give Me S'more Muffins

2 cups graham cracker crumbs
⅓ cup sugar
⅓ cup mini semisweet chocolate chips
2 teaspoons baking powder
¾ cup milk
1 egg
24 milk chocolate candy kisses, unwrapped
2 cups mini marshmallows

1. Preheat oven to 350°F. Line 24 mini (1¾-inch) muffin cups with foil baking cups.

2. Combine graham cracker crumbs, sugar, chocolate chips and baking powder in medium bowl. Whisk milk and egg in small bowl; stir into crumb mixture until well blended. Spoon batter into prepared muffin cups, filling about half full. Press chocolate kiss into center of each cup. Press 4 marshmallows into top of each muffin around chocolate kiss.

3. Bake 10 to 12 minutes or until marshmallows are lightly browned. Cool muffins in pans on wire racks 10 minutes. Remove to racks; cool completely.

Makes about 2 dozen mini muffins

Berry Filled Muffins

1 package DUNCAN HINES® Bakery-Style Wild Maine Blueberry
    Muffin Mix
1 egg
½ cup water
¼ cup strawberry jam
2 tablespoons sliced natural almonds

1. Preheat oven to 400°F. Place 8 (2½-inch) paper or foil liners in muffin cups; set aside.

2. Rinse blueberries from Mix with cold water and drain.

3. Empty muffin mix into bowl. Break up any lumps. Add egg and water. Stir until moistened, about 50 strokes. Fill cups half full with batter.

4. Fold blueberries into jam. Spoon on top of batter in each cup. Spread gently. Cover with remaining batter. Sprinkle with almonds. Bake at 400°F for 17 to 20 minutes or until set and golden brown. Cool in pan 5 to 10 minutes. Loosen carefully before removing from pan.

Makes 8 muffins

Give Me S'more Muffins

Pineapple Carrot Raisin Muffins

  2 cups all-purpose flour
  1 cup sugar
1½ teaspoons baking powder
  1 teaspoon ground cinnamon
  1 can (8 ounces) DOLE® Crushed Pineapple, undrained
  2 eggs
 ½ cup (1 stick) butter or margarine, melted
  1 cup DOLE® Seedless or Golden Raisins
 ½ cup shredded DOLE® Carrots

• Combine flour, sugar, baking powder and cinnamon in large bowl.

• Add undrained pineapple, eggs, butter, raisins and carrots; stir just until blended.

• Spoon evenly into 36 mini muffin cups sprayed with nonstick vegetable cooking spray.

• Bake at 375°F. 15 to 20 minutes or until toothpick inserted into centers comes out clean. Remove muffins from pans to wire racks to cool.   *Makes 36 mini muffins*

For 2½-inch muffins: Spoon batter into 2½-inch muffin pans instead of mini muffin pans. Bake as directed for 20 to 25 minutes. Cool as directed.

Prep Time: 20 minutes
Bake Time: 20 minutes

Banana Peanut Butter Chip Muffins

    2 cups all-purpose flour
    ¾ cup sugar
    2 teaspoons baking powder
    ½ teaspoon baking soda
    ¼ teaspoon salt
    1 cup mashed ripe bananas (about 2 large)
    ½ cup (1 stick) butter, melted
    2 eggs, beaten
    ⅓ cup buttermilk
 1½ teaspoons vanilla
    1 cup peanut butter chips
    ½ cup chopped peanuts

1. Preheat oven to 375°F. Grease 15 standard (2½-inch) muffins cups or line with paper baking cups.

2. Combine flour, sugar, baking powder, baking soda and salt in large bowl. Beat bananas, butter, eggs, buttermilk and vanilla in medium bowl until well blended.

3. Add banana mixture to flour mixture; stir just until blended. Gently fold in peanut butter chips. Spoon batter into prepared muffin cups, filling three-fourths full. Sprinkle with chopped peanuts.

4. Bake 20 minutes or until toothpick inserted into centers comes out clean. Cool 2 minutes in pan. Remove from pan; cool completely on wire racks. Serve warm or at room temperature.   *Makes 15 muffins*

Substitute a mixture of chocolate and peanut butter chips for the peanut butter chips. The combination makes three great flavors in one muffin.

Banana Peanut Butter Chip Muffins

Pies & Tarts

Honey Pumpkin Pie

1 **can (16 ounces) solid pack pumpkin**
1 **cup evaporated low-fat milk**
¾ **cup honey**
3 **eggs, slightly beaten**
2 **tablespoons all-purpose flour**
1 **teaspoon ground cinnamon**
½ **teaspoon ground ginger**
½ **teaspoon rum extract**
   Pastry for single 9-inch pie crust

Combine pumpkin, evaporated milk, honey, eggs, flour, cinnamon, ginger and rum
extract in large bowl; beat until well blended. Pour into pastry-lined 9-inch pie plate.
Bake at 400°F 45 minutes or until knife inserted near center comes out clean.

Makes 8 servings

Favorite recipe from **National Honey Board**

Chocolate Walnut Toffee Tart

2 cups all-purpose flour
1¼ cups plus 3 tablespoons sugar, divided
¾ cup (1½ sticks) cold butter, cut into pieces
2 egg yolks
1¼ cups whipping cream
1 teaspoon ground cinnamon
2 teaspoons vanilla
2 cups coarsely chopped walnuts
1¼ cups semisweet chocolate chips or chunks, divided

1. Preheat oven to 325°F. Place flour and 3 tablespoons sugar in food processor; pulse just until mixed. Scatter butter over flour mixture; process 20 seconds. Add egg yolks; process 10 seconds (mixture may be crumbly).

2. Transfer dough to ungreased 10-inch tart pan with removable bottom or 9- or 10-inch pie pan. Press dough firmly and evenly into pan. Bake 10 minutes or until surface is no longer shiny.

3. *Increase oven temperature to 375°F.* Place piece of foil in bottom of oven to catch any spills. Combine remaining 1¼ cups sugar, cream and cinnamon in large saucepan; bring to a boil over medium-high heat. Reduce heat to low; simmer 10 minutes, stirring frequently. Remove from heat and stir in vanilla.

4. Sprinkle walnuts and 1 cup chocolate chips evenly over partially baked crust. Pour cream mixture over top. Bake 35 to 40 minutes or until filling is bubbly and crust is lightly browned. Cool completely in pan on wire rack.

5. Place remaining ¼ cup chocolate chips in small resealable food storage bag. Microwave on HIGH 20 seconds; knead bag until chocolate is melted. Cut small hole in one corner of bag; drizzle chocolate over tart.   *Makes 12 servings*

Note: Tart may be made up to 5 days in advance. Cover with plastic wrap and store at room temperature.

Prep Time: 25 minutes
Bake Time: 40 minutes

Rustic Plum Tart

¼ cup (½ stick) plus 1 tablespoon butter, divided
3 cups plum wedges (about 6 plums, see tip)
¼ cup granulated sugar
½ cup all-purpose flour
½ cup uncooked old-fashioned or quick oats
¼ cup packed brown sugar
½ teaspoon ground cinnamon
¼ teaspoon salt
1 egg
1 teaspoon water
1 refrigerated pie crust (half of 15-ounce package)
1 tablespoon chopped crystallized ginger

1. Preheat oven to 425°F. Line baking sheet with parchment paper.

2. Melt 1 tablespoon butter in large skillet over high heat. Add plums; cook and stir about 3 minutes or until plums begin to break down. Stir in granulated sugar; cook 1 minute or until juices have thickened. Remove from heat; set aside.

3. Combine flour, oats, brown sugar, cinnamon and salt in medium bowl. Cut in remaining ¼ cup butter with pastry blender or two knives until mixture resembles coarse crumbs.

4. Beat egg and water in small bowl. Unroll pie crust on prepared baking sheet. Brush crust lightly with egg mixture. Sprinkle with ¼ cup oat mixture, leaving 2-inch border around edge of crust. Spoon plums over oat mixture, leaving juices in skillet. Sprinkle with ginger. Fold crust up around plums, overlapping as necessary. Sprinkle with remaining oat mixture. Brush edge of crust with egg mixture.

5. Bake 25 minutes or until golden brown. Cool slightly before serving.

Makes 8 servings

For this recipe, use dark reddish-purple plums and cut the fruit into 8 wedges.

Praline Pumpkin Tart

1¼ **cups all-purpose flour**
1 **tablespoon granulated sugar**
¾ **teaspoon salt, divided**
¼ **cup shortening**
¼ **cup (½ stick) butter**
3 to 4 **tablespoons cold water**
1 **can (15 ounces) solid-pack pumpkin (not pumpkin pie filling)**
1 **can (12 ounces) evaporated milk**
⅔ **cup packed brown sugar**
2 **eggs**
1 **teaspoon ground cinnamon, plus additional for garnish**
½ **teaspoon ground ginger**
¼ **teaspoon ground cloves**
   Praline Topping (page 73)
   Sweetened Whipped Cream (page 73)
   Pecan halves (optional)

1. Combine flour, granulated sugar and ¼ teaspoon salt in large bowl. Cut in shortening and butter using pastry blender or two knives until mixture is crumbly.

2. Sprinkle flour mixture with water, 1 tablespoon at a time. Toss with fork until mixture holds together. Shape into ball; wrap in plastic wrap. Refrigerate about 1 hour or until chilled.

3. Roll out dough on lightly floured surface into circle 1 inch larger than inverted 10-inch tart pan with removable bottom or 1½ inches larger than inverted 9-inch pie plate. Transfer dough to tart pan or pie plate; cover with plastic wrap and refrigerate 30 minutes.

4. Preheat oven to 400°F. Pierce crust with tines of fork at ¼-inch intervals. Line tart pan with foil; fill with dried beans, uncooked rice or ceramic pie weights. Bake 10 minutes or until set. Remove from oven; gently remove foil lining and beans. Return to oven and bake 5 minutes or until very light brown. Cool completely on wire rack.

5. Beat pumpkin, evaporated milk, brown sugar, eggs, cinnamon, remaining ½ teaspoon salt, ginger and cloves in large bowl with electric mixer at low speed. Pour into cooled tart crust. Bake 35 minutes.

6. Prepare Praline Topping. Sprinkle topping over center of tart, leaving 1½-inch rim around edge of tart. Bake 15 minutes or until knife inserted 1 inch from center comes out clean.

7. Cool completely on wire rack. Prepare Sweetened Whipped Cream and pipe decoratively around edge of tart. Sprinkle additional cinnamon over whipped cream. Garnish with pecan halves.

Makes 8 servings

Praline Topping

⅓ **cup packed brown sugar**
⅓ **cup chopped pecans**
⅓ **cup uncooked quick oats**
1 **tablespoon butter or margarine, softened**

Place brown sugar, pecans and oats in small bowl. Cut in butter with pastry blender or two knives until coarse crumbs form.

Makes about 1 cup

Sweetened Whipped Cream

1 **cup heavy cream**
2 **tablespoons powdered sugar**
½ **teaspoon vanilla**

Chill large bowl, beaters and cream before whipping. Place cream, powdered sugar and vanilla into chilled bowl and beat with electric mixer at high speed until soft peaks form. *Do not overbeat.* Refrigerate until ready to serve.

Makes about 2 cups

Sweet 'n' Spicy Pecan Pie

Prepared pie crust for one 9-inch pie
3 **eggs**
1 **cup dark corn syrup**
½ **cup dark brown sugar**
¼ **cup (½ stick) butter or margarine, melted**
1 **tablespoon Original TABASCO® brand Pepper Sauce**
1½ **cups pecans, coarsely chopped**
Whipped cream (optional)

Preheat oven to 425°F. Place pie crust in 9-inch pie plate; flute edge of crust.

Beat eggs lightly in large bowl. Stir in corn syrup, brown sugar, butter and TABASCO® Sauce; mix well. Place pecans in prepared pie crust; pour filling over pecans. Bake 15 minutes.

Reduce oven to 350°F. Bake pie 40 minutes or until knife inserted 1 inch from edge comes out clean. Cool pie on wire rack. Serve with whipped cream, if desired.

Makes 8 servings

Apple & Cherry Pie

2 cups all-purpose flour
½ cup plus 2½ tablespoons sugar, divided
½ teaspoon salt
3 tablespoons butter or margarine
3 tablespoons shortening
5 to 6 tablespoons ice water
1 tablespoon cider vinegar
½ cup dried cherries
¼ cup apple juice
1 tablespoon cornstarch
2¼ teaspoons ground cinnamon, divided
6 cups red baking apples, preferably Jonagold or Golden Delicious
1 teaspoon vanilla
1 egg white, well beaten

1. Combine flour, 2 tablespoons sugar and salt in large bowl. Cut in butter and shortening with pastry blender or two knives until mixture resembles coarse crumbs. Stir in 4 tablespoons water and vinegar with fork. Add additional water, 1 tablespoon at a time, until mixture forms soft dough. Divide dough into thirds. Shape 1 piece into disc; wrap in plastic wrap. Combine remaining 2 pieces dough, forming larger disc; wrap in plastic wrap. Refrigerate 30 minutes.

2. Preheat oven to 375°F. Combine cherries and apple juice in small microwavable bowl; microwave on HIGH 1½ minutes. Let stand 15 minutes to plump cherries. Combine ½ cup sugar, cornstarch and 2 teaspoons cinnamon in large bowl; mix well. Peel and thinly slice apples. Add to bowl with vanilla; toss to combine.

3. Coat 9-inch pie plate with nonstick cooking spray. Roll larger disc of dough into 12-inch circle, ⅛-inch thick on lightly floured surface. Transfer pastry to prepared pie plate. Spoon apple mixture into pastry. Roll smaller disc of dough to ⅛-inch thickness. Cut dough into ½-inch strips. Place strips over filling and weave into lattice design. Trim ends of lattice strips; push edge of lower crust over ends of lattice strips. Seal and flute edge.

4. Brush pastry with egg white. Combine remaining ½ tablespoon sugar and ¼ teaspoon cinnamon; sprinkle over pie. Bake 45 to 50 minutes or until apples are tender and crust is golden brown. Cool 30 minutes. Serve warm or at room temperature.

Makes 8 servings

Tip: If the pie crust is browning too quickly, cover the edges with strips of aluminum foil. Or, cut the bottom out of a foil pie pan and invert it over the pie.

Apple & Cherry Pie

Classic Apple Pie

  1 package (15 ounces) refrigerated pie crusts (2 crusts)
  6 cups sliced Granny Smith, Crispin or other firm-fleshed apples
  ½ cup sugar
  1 tablespoon cornstarch
  2 teaspoons lemon juice
  ½ teaspoon *each* ground cinnamon and vanilla
  ⅛ teaspoon *each* salt, ground nutmeg and ground cloves
  1 tablespoon whipping cream

1. Preheat oven to 350°F. Unfold one pie crust; press into 9-inch pie dish. (Refrigerate remaining pie crust while preparing apples.)

2. Combine apples, sugar, cornstarch, lemon juice, cinnamon, vanilla, salt, nutmeg and cloves in large bowl; mix well. Pour into prepared crust. Place second crust over apples; crimp around edge to seal crusts together.

3. Cut 4 slits in top crust; brush top crust with cream. Bake 40 minutes or until apples are tender and crust is golden brown. Cool slightly before serving.

Makes 8 servings

Country Pecan Pie

     Pastry for single 9-inch pie crust
  1¼ cups dark corn syrup
   4 eggs
  ½ cup packed light brown sugar
  ¼ cup (½ stick) butter or margarine, melted
   2 teaspoons all-purpose flour
  1½ teaspoons vanilla
  1½ cups pecan halves

1. Preheat oven to 350°F. Roll pastry on lightly floured surface to form 13-inch circle. Fit into 9-inch pie plate. Trim edges; flute. Set aside.

2. Beat corn syrup, eggs, brown sugar and butter in large bowl with electric mixer at medium speed 2 to 3 minutes or until well blended. Stir in flour and vanilla until blended. Pour into unbaked pie crust. Arrange pecans on top.

3. Bake 40 to 45 minutes until center of filling is puffed and golden brown. Cool completely on wire rack.

Makes 8 servings

Classic Apple Pie

The publisher would like to thank the companies and organizations listed below for the use of their recipes and photographs in this publication.

California Dried Plum Board

Cream of Wheat® Cereal

Dole Food Company, Inc.

Duncan Hines® and Moist Deluxe® are registered trademarks of Pinnacle Foods Corp.

The Hershey Company

© Mars, Incorporated 2010

McIlhenny Company (TABASCO® brand Pepper Sauce)

National Honey Board

Nestlé USA